# ⚊ SAIJUTSU ⚊

## TRADITIONAL OKINAWAN WEAPON ART

D1637401

# ~ SAIJUTSU ~

## TRADITIONAL OKINAWAN WEAPON ART

Katsumi Murakami

BROOKLINE PUBLIC LIBRARY

Tuttle Publishing

Boston ~ Rutland, Vermont ~ Tokyo

796.8
Murakami
2000

This edition published in 2000 by Tuttle Publishing, an imprint of Periplus Editions (HK) Ltd., with editorial offices at 153 Milk Street, Boston, Massachusetts, 02109.

Copyright © 2000 Katsumi Murakami

3 1712 00791 9270

All rights reserved. No part of this publication may be reproduced or utilized in any form or by any means, electronic or mechanical, including photocopying, recording, or by any information storage and retrieval system, without prior written permission from Tuttle Publishing.

Library of Congress Cataloging-in-Publication Data in Process
ISBN: 0-8048-3244-7


Distributed by


North America
Tuttle Publishing
Distribution Center
Airport Industrial Park
364 Innovation Drive
North Clarendon, VT 05759-9436
Tel: (802) 773-8930
Tel: (800) 526-2778
Fax: (802) 773-6993

Japan
Tuttle Publishing
RK Building, 2nd Floor
2-13-10 Shimo-Meguro, Meguro-Ku
Tokyo 153 0064
Tel: (03) 5437-0171
Tel: (03) 5437-0755


Asia Pacific
Berkeley Books Pte Ltd
5 Little Road #08-01
Singapore 536983
Tel: (65) 280-1330
Fax: (65) 280-6290


05 04 03 02 01 00    9 8 7 6 5 4 3 2 1

Printed in the United States of America

# Contents

# — FOREWORD —

*Karatedo* originated in Okinawa, but has become a cosmopolitan sport that has spread to all areas of the world. Nevertheless, Ryukyu *kobudo*, karatedoís sister martial art from the same Okinawa, is still only known by a small number of people. Even within Japan, it has not become widespread. Of course, it is almost unknown outside of Japan. From old times in Okinawa, the masters of karatedo were also masters of Ryukyu kobudo. Karatedo and Ryukyu kobudo are like two wheels that belong to the same cart. If you study Ryukyu kobudo, you can understand karatedo, too. Karate is not just for sports. I hope that you look for the way of karate, which is essentially *budo*. At the same time, followers of karatedo should also study Ryukyu kobudo. In this book, I am going to focus upon Ryukyu kobudoís *Saijutsu* and its basic *kata*, the practice forms. I hope that this book can help those who love karatedo, as well as those who follow other martial arts. Finally, I want to express my deepest thanks to my student Mr. Bruce Vail and his colleague Mr. Kifuji Hiroyuki, for good-heartedly translating this book into English; to Mr. Joe Swift for his assistance in the publication of this book; and to Mr. George Donahue of Tuttle Publishing for agreeing to publish my work.

# INTRODUCTION

## ABOUT SAIJUTSU

*Saijutsu*, the art of the sai, is one of the martial arts that make up Ryukyu *Kobudo*. Ryukyu Kobudo is the collective term for the ancient martial arts of Okinawa that make use of old-style weapons. The roots and time of origin of saijutsu are about the same as those of *karatedo* and the other martial arts among Ryukyu Kobudo, including *bojutsu* (the art of the staff), *tonfajutsu* (the art of utilizing the wooden handles of a rice-grinding tool), *nichogamajutsu* (the art of using two farming sickles), and so forth.

In brief, the civil measures of Okinawan King Sho Hashi, and later the policies of the Satsuma rulers included a hasty confiscation of swords and spears and other weapons. These actions caused Okinawan people to earnestly study and train in the various martial arts left to them.

Past and present, great masters of saijutsu included *Bushi* Matsumura, Tsuken Shitahaku, Hama Higa, Chatan Yara, Tawada, Ishikawa-Guwa no Kekere-Ou, and Kaneko *Ufuchiku*, among others.

Saijutsu uses a weapon similar to the *jitte* used by the *torigata* of the Japanese mainland. The torigata were the equivalent of today's police. In Ryukyu, however, it seems that the torigata used the *sai*. The jitte had a fork on one side and could be used to deal with a sword or staff by stopping it with a scissoring action of the fork. The sai was different in that each had two forks. Saijutsu uses a pair of sai which are handled with both hands. They can be handled with perfect freedom for both offense and defense.

At the present time, Ryukyu kobudo principally revolves around bojutsu (the art of the staff) and saijutsu. While karatedo is a martial art that uses the empty hands to defend against an enemy, the martial arts of Ryukyu kobudo defend against an enemy by using weapons. Among the core of martial artists from the Ryukyu islands, from early historical times, these two martial arts (karate and kobudo) have been prominent. Therefore, karate and kobudo are like two wheels of a cart. They are sister martial arts.

Recently, Ryukyu kobudo has experienced a revival under the students of Yabiku Moden Sensei. One of those followers, Taira Shinken Sensei, passed on the heart of Yabiku's teachings to a figure who was to become the successor after Taira Sensei's death. The figure who was to inherit this path through his diligent study and devotion was Inoue Motokatsu Sensei.

The early developers and later masters preserved various *kata*, or practice forms. These kata were designed to cultivate mastery through repetitive practice and training.

# The Relationship Between Sai and Karate, and Its Value

Saijutsu is an art of utilizing weapons, while karate is the art of using the limbs as weapons. Nevertheless, the use of the sai is applied to karate techniques, as the sai can be considered extensions of the hands. By practicing the elaborate manipulations of saijutsu, we also exercise and stimulate the cerebrum. Saijutsu also trains the wrists and arms, thereby making one's karate punches and strikes more powerful. It goes without saying that manipulating the heavy sai for the purposes of offense or defense can train the whole body. Overall, sai training is a great help in developing karate techniques. It is very important for everybody who practices karate to develop a strong body. For that purpose, I think that bodybuilding through weight training is one good training practice. I would also suggest doing sai training to complement the bodybuilding. Although I have mentioned that sai can be considered to be part of our hands, it is so important that I want to emphasize this point again. You can manipulate the sai as if they were part of your own hands. However, you need a lot of practice to reach that stage.

We sometimes speak of "masterful performance." So-called "living national treasures" have been improving their skills for a long time. They try to use every means to fine-tune their technique which is really beyond that of ordinary people. This can be achieved only by daily practice. The same thing applies to the martial arts. If you continue to practice every day, someday you will be able to master the techniques that are beyond ordinary people's ability. The main principle of the practice of sai or karate should be hard training. This training produces the same feeling that believers experience when they perform their daily practice of praying. Let me quote the words of Dogen, a famous Zen Buddhist teacher: "To learn Buddhism is to learn oneself. To learn oneself is to forget oneself." To forget oneself is to be tested in an established way. By testing ourselves in an established way, we are also encouraged to try very hard. If we try very hard in the training of the sai or karate, we will forget ourselves. It also means to learn ourselves, and to learn ourselves entails learning Buddhism. In short, training in sai or karate leads to a spiritual awakening.

The karate that is regarded as a sport has age limitations whereas the karate that is regarded as a martial art requires no retirement. You must be able to train yourself even when you are old, if you are to master the karate of martial arts. Whether you are studying sai or karate, the core of the training should be practicing kata. The older you grow, the more skilled you should be, and the simpler it should be for you to distinguish yourself. You should be able to enjoy the training in forms of sai or karate until the very end of your life. In addition to the healthy body we can develop through physical activity of sai or karate training, we can become one with the atoms of the universe, the core of everything, and by doing that, we try to merge ourselves with the universe, resulting in mental as well as physical well-being.

No matter how much nutrition human beings get from food, unless they move their bodies to absorb the essence, they will never be healthy in the truest sense of the word. In other words, people could very well be healthy without enough food by assimilating essence. All creatures, including human beings, came from this essence, so all creatures are actually harmonized in nature.

We have to practice karate or sai based upon the idea of harmonizing with nature to absorb the active essence. In other words, you should practice by merging with the essence of the universe, which will make you feel very comfortable. This can be true, not only for karate or sai practice, but also for other kinds of martial arts, such as the ancient arts of *bo, kama, nunchaku, tonfa, taijiquan, baguazhang, xingyiquan,* and so forth. These martial arts are wonderful art forms that man has invented. These art forms enrich our lives and give them direction. I really hope this heritage will be handed down to the next generation. We should continue the maintenance of our health.

The important part of our culture should be handed down from generation to generation. It is true not only in Japan but also in other countries, that the old culture is handed down to the next generation, and so the culture is preserved. This is a very wonderful tradition, but very difficult to maintain.

Some people practice such arts as flower arrangement, the tea ceremony, or *Noh*, which have traditions that date back for centuries. The same is true for the martial arts.

As for the ancient Japanese martial arts, there is a traditional form that has more than two centuries of history. It is very difficult to hand down a culture to the next generation. The important point is for the ones who are responsible for passing on the culture to preserve the culture, polish it, and find good successors to spread it.

The same thing can be said of karate or sai. It is very important to endeavor to preserve it and hand it down for future generations. In the art that is ceaselessly preserved is the spirit of generations of warriors. For example, when you talk about the karate of the *Shorin* school, you must consider the stream of tradition in which Matsumura Sokon practiced the form and handed it down to Itosu Anko and Chibana Choshin, who made a great effort and handed it down to us. As for the karate of the *To-on* school, the karate that was originated by Higaonna Kanryo was taught to Kyoda Juhatsu, who taught it to us. The same is true of sai. Before us, Taira Shinken practiced the form and taught it to Inoue Motokatsu, to hand it down to us. Before Taira Shinken, there were such warriors as Hama Higa, Chatan Yara, Yakaa of Hama Udun, Kouraguwa, Tsuken Shitahaku, and Tawada, who endeavored to master the forms.

We can see that the figures who practiced the forms of karate or sai kept alive the spirit of their teachers. The stream of spirit preserves the tradition as well as the stream of life. There is absolute truth in this. The basic kata 1, 2, and 3 (*Sai Kihongata Ichi, Ni,* and *San*) were invented by me. I very much hope that many people practice these forms as introductory forms to the traditional kata of the sai.

## The Lineage of Saijutsu

The art of saijutsu was passed down in the following order:

Kaneko Ufuchiku

↓

Yabiku Moden

↓

Taira Shinken

↓

Inoue Motokatsu

↓

Murakami Katsumi (the author).

## The Kata of Saijutsu

The kata being preserved and passed on at the author's *Shorinkan dojo* include *Kihongata Ichi, Kihongata Ni, Kihongata San, Tawada no Sai Ichi, Matsumura no Sai, Tsuken Shitahaku no Sai, Hama Higa no Sai, Tawada no Sai Ni, Chatan Yara no Sai, Hama Udun Yakaa no Sai, Jigen no Sai, Kogusuku no Sai,* and *Hantagawa Kouraguwa no Sai.*

# ONE

# SAIJUTSU KIHONGATA ICHI

*Enbusen* (floor design or performance pattern):

**East**

**North**                                             **South**

**West**

**1**

*Hold both sai in the left hand,
facing east, standing in
**musubi-dachi** stance.*

**2**

*Bow.*

**3**

Hold the pair of sai with one in each hand. Cross the sai in front of the chest. Follow by moving both sai downward to the sides of the body, while moving the left and the right foot into **hachiji-dachi** stance. Assume the **hiraki-yoi** position (hinged ready stance).

**4**

Slide-step (the same footwork as in karate's **oi-tsuki**, lunge punch) to the east with the left foot, and perform a left reverse sai middle-level thrust.

**5**

*In the same position, follow with a right reverse sai middle-level thrust.*

**6**

*Slide-step to the east with the right foot and right reverse sai middle-level thrust.*

**7**

*In the same position, follow with a left reverse sai middle-level thrust.*

**8**

*Step to the east with the left foot, and perform a left reverse sai middle-level thrust.*

**9**

*In the same position, follow with a right reverse sai middle-level thrust.*

**10**

*Move the left foot to twist the body to face the opposite direction (west). Stand on the left leg with the right leg raised and execute a right sai downward block.*

**11**

*Drop the right leg. Bring the handle of the right sai to the waist. With the left sai, perform an upper strike.*

**12**

*Stand on the right leg with the left leg raised and execute a left sai downward block.*

**13**

*Drop the left leg and perform a right upper sai strike.*

**14**

*Change to a left cat stance and perform a left reverse sai inside middle block. Bring the right sai in the reverse position to the waist.*

**15**

*Move the right foot forward.
Perform a right reverse sai
middle-level thrust.*

**16**

*Change to a right cat stance.
Perform a right reverse sai
inside middle block.*

**17**

*Step forward with the left leg. Perform a left reverse sai middle-level thrust.*

**18**

*Change to a left cat stance. Perform a left reverse sai inside middle block.*

**19**

*Move the right foot forward.
Perform a right reverse sai
middle-level thrust.*

**20**

*From the same position, follow
with a left reverse sai
middle-level thrust.*

**21**

*Move the right leg and turn to the left, changing to face the front (east). Use both sai to perform a reverse sai downward block.*

**22**

*From the same position, move both sai to a vertical position with both arms extended horizontally to the sides in the **yama-gamae** position (shaped like the ideogram "yama" for mountain).*

**23**

*Move the right leg to the right (south) to assume a left cat stance facing to the left (north). Perform a left reverse sai inside middle block. Right reverse sai to waist.*

**24**

*From that position, perform a right reverse sai middle-level thrust.*

**25**

*In the same position, left reverse sai middle-level thrust.*

**26**

*From that position, left reverse sai upper-level block and right reverse sai to the waist.*

**27**

*From that position, right sai upper-level strike. Left reverse sai to the waist.*

**28**

*From that position, left reverse sai middle-level thrust.*

**29**

*From the same position, right reverse sai middle-level thrust.*

**30**

*Move the left leg and turn to the right, facing the back (south) in a right cat stance. Perform a right reverse sai inside-middle block. Left reverse sai to the waist.*

**31**

*From that position, left reverse sai middle-level thrust*

**32**

*From that position, right reverse sai middle-level thrust*

**33**

*From that position, right reverse sai upper-level block. Left reverse sai to waist.*

**34**

*From that position, left upper-level strike. Right reverse sai to waist.*

**35**

*From the same position, right reverse sai middle-level thrust.*

**36**

*From the same position, left reverse sai middle-level thrust.*

**37**

*Move the right leg to the front (east). Using both sai, upper-level strike.*

**38**

*Stepping forward with the front foot and dragging the back foot, double-sai side strike.*

**39**

*Stepping forward again with the front foot and dragging the back foot, double-sai thrust to the front.*

**40**

*Move the right leg and turn to the left to face the back (west) in a cat stance. Left reverse sai inside-middle block.*

**41**

*Step ahead with the right leg and right reverse sai middle-level thrust.*

**42**

*Change to right cat stance. Right reverse sai inside-middle block.*

**43**

*Step forward with the left leg. Left reverse sai middle-level thrust.*

**44**

*From that position, right reverse sai middle-level thrust.*

**45**

*Stepping forward with the front foot and dragging the back foot, double-sai lower thrust.*

**46**

*Move the right leg and turn the body to the left to face the front (east) on the **enbusen**. With both sai, upper-level cross block.*

**47**

*Pull the left leg back to return to*
***yoi,*** *the ready position.*

**48**

*Hold both sai in the left hand.*
*Change to musubi-dachi. Bow.*

# T W O
## SAIJUTSU KIHONGATA NI

In order to prepare the learner for the more advanced, ancient kata of saijutsu, this author has devised three basic forms, known collectively as Saijutsu Kihongata. Introducing the fundamental defensive and offensive techniques of saijutsu, these three basic practice forms are useful in learning to manipulate this graceful, yet difficult weapon.

**1**

*Bow.*

**2**

*Assume the ready position.*

**3**

*Step forward with the left leg into a left cat stance. Left reverse sai inside block.*

**4**

*From that position, right reverse sai middle-level thrust.*

**5**

*Move the right leg forward into a cat stance. Right reverse sai inside block.*

**6**

*From that position, left reverse sai middle-level thrust.*

**7**

*Step forward with the left leg into a left cat stance. Left reverse sai inside block.*

**8**

*From that position, right reverse sai middle-level thrust.*

**9**

*From that position, left reverse sai middle-level thrust.*

**10**

*Step forward with the front foot and drag the back foot. Left reverse sai upper block. Right reverse sai middle thrust.*

**11**

*Step with the right foot to turn to the left facing the back (west) of the enbusen. Lower both sai down into the **kaki-wake** position.*

**12**

*From the same position, lower both sai down to the sides in the **kaki-otoshi** position.*

**13**

*Move the right leg forward. Right sai upper strike. Left reverse sai downward block.*

**14**

*Step ahead with the left leg. Left upper strike. Right reverse sai downward block.*

**15**

*Step ahead with the right leg.
Right reverse sai middle-level
thrust.*

**16**

*From the same position, left
reverse sai middle-level thrust.*

**17**

*From the same position, right
reverse sai middle-level thrust.*

**18**

*Move the left leg toward the
left (south). Left reverse sai
inside block.*

**19**

*In the same position, right reverse sai middle-level thrust.*

**20**

*In the same position, left reverse sai middle-level thrust.*

**21**

*In the same position, left reverse sai upper block.*

**22**

*In the same position, right sai upper strike.*

**23**

*In the same position, left reverse sai middle-level thrust.*

**24**

*In the same position, right reverse sai middle-level thrust.*

**25**

*In the same position, left reverse sai upper block.*

**26**

*Turn to the right to face the back (north). Right reverse sai inside block.*

**27**

*In the same position, left reverse sai middle-level thrust.*

**28**

*In the same position, right reverse sai middle-level thrust.*

**29**

*In the same position, right reverse sai upper block.*

**30**

*In the same position, left sai upper strike.*

**31**

*In the same position, right reverse sai middle-level thrust.*

**32**

*In the same position, left reverse sai middle-level thrust.*

**33**

*In the same position, right reverse sai upper block.*

**34**

*Move the right leg to the front (east) of the enbusen, to change to face the back (west). Left reverse sai middle block.*

**35**

*From that position, right reverse sai middle-level thrust.*

**36**

*From that position, left reverse sai middle-level thrust.*

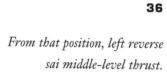

**37**

*From that position, left reverse sai upper block.*

**38**

*From that position, right sai upper-level strike.*

**39**

*From that position, left reverse sai middle-level thrust.*

**40**

*From that position, right reverse sai middle-level thrust.*

**41**

*From that position, left reverse sai upper block.*

**42**

*Turn to the right to face the back (east). Right sai upper-level strike.*

**43**

*From that position, right reverse sai downward block.*

**44**

*From that position, left reverse sai middle-level thrust.*

**45**

*From that position, right reverse sai middle-level thrust.*

**46**

*From that position, left reverse sai middle-level thrust.*

**47**

From that position, right reverse sai upper block.

**48**

Turn to the left to face the back (west). Left sai upper-level strike.

**49**

*From that position, left reverse sai downward block.*

**50**

*From that position, right reverse sai middle-level thrust.*

**51**

*From that position, left reverse sai middle-level thrust.*

**52**

*From that position, right reverse sai middle-level thrust.*

**53**

*From that position, left reverse sai upper block.*

**54**

*Turn to the right to face the back (east). Right sai upper-level strike.*

**55**

*Step and pivot toward the left, making a 360-degree turn, and perform a double-sai lower level cross block.*

**56**

*From that position, double-sai upper-level cross block.*

**57**

*Step with the front foot and drag the back foot. Double-sai upper-level strike.*

**58**

*Step again with the front foot and drag the back foot. Double-sai thrust.*

**59**

*Pull back the right leg. Left reverse sai inside block.*

**60**

*From that position, right reverse sai middle-level thrust.*

**61**

*Pull back the left leg. Right reverse sai inside block.*

**62**

*From that position, left reverse sai middle-level thrust.*

**63**

*Pull back the right leg. Left reverse sai upper block.*

**64**

*From that position, right reverse sai middle-level thrust.*

**65**

*From that position, left reverse sai middle-level thrust.*

**66**

*From that position, right reverse sai middle-level thrust.*

**67**

*Return to ready position.*

**68**

*Bow.*

# THREE

# SAIJUTSU KIHONGATA SAN

As with all martial arts, a strong grasp of the fundamentals is vital to gaining understanding of the advanced techniques. It is hoped that these three basic kata, devised by the author, help the readers on their way to mastery of saijutsu.

**1**

*Bow.*

**2**

*Assume the ready position.*

**3**

*Step back with the right foot. Left reverse sai upper block.*

**4**

*Step back again with the right foot. Left reverse sai inside block.*

**5**

*Change directions to face the right (south). Standing on the left leg (right leg raised), right sai downward block.*

**6**

*Drop the right leg and at the same time perform a right upper sai strike.*

**7**

*Slide the left leg forward. Left reverse sai middle-level thrust.*

**8**

*From that position, right reverse sai middle-level thrust.*

**9**

*Turn to the left to face the back (north). Standing on the right leg (left leg raised), left sai downward block.*

**10**

*Drop the left leg and at the same time perform a left upper sai strike.*

**11**

*Slide the right leg forward. Right reverse sai middle-level thrust.*

**12**

*From that position, left reverse sai middle-level thrust.*

**13**

*Move the right foot toward the right (east) to bring it together with the left foot. Facing the west, stand on the right leg (left leg raised). Left sai downward block beside the raised left leg.*

**14**

*Drop the left leg and at the same time perform a left upper sai strike.*

**15**

*Slide the right leg forward. Right reverse sai middle-level thrust.*

**16**

*From that position, left reverse sai middle-level thrust.*

**17**

*Turn to the left to face the front (east). Left reverse sai upper block.*

**18**

*Step forward with the right leg. Right sai upper strike.*

**19**

*Step forward with the left leg. Left reverse sai middle-level thrust.*

**20**

*Pull the left leg back. Right reverse sai inside block.*

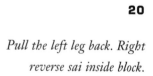

**21**

*Pull the right leg back. Left reverse sai inside block.*

**22**

*Pull the left leg back. Right reverse sai inside block.*

**23**

*Step with the right foot to turn to the left, facing the enbusen's front (east). Left sai upper strike.*

**24**

*Slide the right leg forward. Right reverse sai middle-level thrust.*

**25**

*Standing on the left leg (right leg raised), perform a right sai downward block.*

**26**

*Drop the right leg back to the ground. Right reverse sai upper block.*

**27**

*Slide the left leg forward. Left reverse sai middle-level thrust.*

**28**

*Standing on the right leg (left leg raised), perform a left sai downward block.*

**29**

*Drop the left leg back to the ground. Left reverse sai upper block.*

**30**

*Slide the right foot forward. Right reverse sai middle thrust.*

**31**

*Standing on the left leg (right leg raised), perform a right sai downward block.*

**32**

*Drop the right leg back to the ground. Right reverse sai upper block.*

**33**

*Step ahead with the left leg. Left reverse sai middle-level thrust.*

**34**

*Step with the left foot to turn to the right, facing the enbusen's back (west). Right reverse sai upper block.*

**35**

*Step ahead with the left leg. Left reverse sai middle-level thrust.*

**36**

*Step ahead with the right leg. Right sai upper strike.*

**37**

*Turn to the left to face the back (east). Left reverse sai upper block.*

**38**

*Step ahead with the right leg. Right reverse sai middle-level thrust.*

**39**

*Step ahead with the left leg. Left sai upper strike.*

**40**

*Turn to the right to face the back (west). Right reverse sai upper block.*

**41**

*Step ahead with the left leg. Left reverse sai middle-level thrust.*

**42**

*Step ahead with the right leg. Right sai middle-level thrust.*

**43**

*Step ahead with the left leg. Left reverse sai middle-level thrust.*

**44**

*Turn to the right to face the back (east). Right sai upper strike.*

**45**

*Step ahead with the left leg.*
*Downward block using both sai.*

**46**

*Step ahead with the front*
*leg and drag the back leg.*
*Double-sai upper strike.*

**47**

*Move the right leg ahead into* **shiko-dachi** *(sumo posture). With the tip of the right sai thrust to the front (east).*

**48**

*In the same position, thrust to the back (west) with a right reverse sai.*

**49**

*From the same position, thrust to the front (east) with the point of the right sai.*

**50**

*Turn to the left toward the west. Left sai upper strike.*

**51**

*Step forward with the right leg.*
*Double-sai downward block.*

**52**

*Step ahead with the front*
*leg and drag the back leg.*
*Double-sai upper strike.*

**53**

*Step with the right leg into shiko-dachi. Thrust to the back (west) with the tip of the left sai.*

**54**

*From the same position, thrust to the front (east) with a left reverse sai.*

**55**

*From the same position, thrust to the back (west) with the point of the left sai.*

**56**

*Turn to the left, stepping with the right leg toward the west, into shiko-dachi. Thrust toward the back (west) with the point of the right sai.*

**57**

*From the same position, thrust toward the front (east) with a right reverse sai.*

**58**

*From the same position, right sai upper strike toward the back (west).*

**59**

*From the same position, left reverse sai thrust toward the back (west).*

**60**

*From the same position, thrust toward the front (east) with the point of the left sai.*

**61**

*From the same position, left reverse sai thrust toward the back (west).*

**62**

*From the same position, left sai upper strike toward the front (east).*

**63**

*From the same position, right reverse sai middle thrust toward the front (east).*

**64**

*Move the right leg into line with the left leg. Return to the ready position (yoi).*

**65**

*Bow.*

# FOUR 小林流
# TAWADA NO SAI ICHI

This kata is believed to be based upon techniques favored and passed down by Bushi Tawada, a famous Kobudo master who lived during the time of Itosu Anko. To differentiate it from the longer Tawada no Sai passed down in the Taira Shinken lineage, this version is called Tawada no Sai Ichi at the author's dojo.

**1**

*Bow.*

**2**

*Assume a ready position.*

**3**

*Step back with the right leg.*
*Right reverse sai downward block.*
*Left reverse sai upper thrust.*

**4**

*Step ahead with the right leg*
*into a cat stance. Left reverse*
*sai inside middle block.*

**5**

*Shift to the left. Turn the left sai over and perform an upper strike.*

**6**

*Turn the left sai over and bring it back to the waist.*

**7**

*Left reverse sai upper-level thrust.*

**8**

*Slide the right leg forward into a cat stance. Turn over the right sai and perform a right upper-level strike.*

**9**

*Turn the right sai back over and return it to the waist.*

**10**

*Right reverse sai upper-level thrust.*

**11**

*Slide the left leg forward into a cat stance. Left reverse sai upper-level block.*

**12**

*Slide the right leg toward the front (east) into a cat stance. Right reverse sai inside-middle block.*

**13**

*Shift the right leg to the south. Turn the right sai over and perform a right upper-level strike.*

**14**

*Turn the right sai back over and return it to the waist.*

**15**

*Right reverse sai upper-level thrust.*

**16**

*Slide the left leg forward into a cat stance. Turn over the left sai and perform a left upper-level strike.*

**17**

*Turn the left sai back over and return it to the waist.*

**18**

*Left reverse sai upper-level thrust.*

**19**

*Slide the right leg forward into a cat stance. Right reverse sai upper-level block.*

**20**

*Step forward (east) with the left leg into a cat stance. Left reverse sai inside middle block.*

**21**

*Slide the right leg forward. Right reverse sai inside middle block.*

**22**

*Pull back the right leg. Left sai down block.*

**23**

*Pull back the left leg. Right sai downward block.*

**24**

*Pull back the right leg. Left sai downward block.*

**25**

*Pull the left leg back. Double-sai downward cross block.*

**26**

*Double upper-level cross block.*

**27**

*Upper-level strike with the right sai.*

**28**

*Turn the right sai over and bring it back to the waist.*

**29**

*Right reverse sai upper-level thrust.*

**30**

*Turn the left sai over and perform a left sai upper-level strike.*

**31**

*Turn the left sai back over and return it to the waist.*

**32**

*Left reverse sai upper-level thrust.*

**33**

*Step forward with the right leg. Turn the right sai over and perform a right upper-level strike.*

**34**

*Turn the right sai back over and return it to the waist.*

**35**

*Right reverse sai upper-level thrust.*

**36**

*Pull back the right leg into a cat stance and perform a left reverse sai downward block.*

**37**

*Move the right leg to the right side (south). Turn the right sai over and perform a right upper-level strike.*

**38**

*Turn the right sai back over and return it to the waist.*

**39**

*Right reverse sai upper-level thrust.*

**40**

*Move the left leg forward. Turn the left sai over and perform a left upper-level strike.*

**41**

*Turn the left sai back over and return it to the waist.*

**42**

*Left reverse sai upper-level thrust.*

**43**

*Move the right leg forward into a right cat stance. Right reverse sai downward block.*

**44**

*Turn to the left (north). Turn over the left sai and perform a left upper-level strike.*

**45**

*Turn the left sai back over and return it to the waist.*

**46**

*Left reverse sai upper-level thrust.*

**47**

*Step forward with the right leg. Turn over the right sai and perform a right upper-level strike.*

**48**

*Turn the right sai back over and return it to the waist.*

**49**

*Right sai upper-level thrust.*

**50**

*Move the left foot forward into a cat stance. Left reverse sai downward block.*

**51**

*Return to ready position.*

**52**

*Bow.*

# FIVE
## MATSUMURA NO SAI

This very rare kata is believed to have been passed down from Bushi Matsumura Sokon, of Shuri. Although better known for his empty hand skills, tradition tells us that Matsumura was also well versed in the weapons associated with the Okinawan martial arts, as well as those of China and Satsuma.

**1**

*Bow.*

**2**

*Assume the ready position.*

**3**

*Pull the right leg one step back. Assume a left cat stance. Move the left hand out to the front and raise the sai. Bring the right sai alongside the top of the left sai.*

**4**

*Advance with the right leg. Left reverse sai inside block.*

**5**

*Advance with the left leg. Right reverse sai inside block.*

**6**

*Advance with the right leg. Left reverse sai inside block.*

**7**

*Assume shiko-dachi stance. With both sai in the yama-gamae position, repel an attack. The body faces to the south.*

**8**

*Return both sai to the waist.*

**9**

*With both sai, perform a double thrust.*

**10**

*Raise the right leg. Bring back both sai. Downward block.*

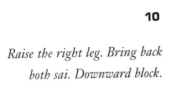

**11**

*Put the right leg down. Move both sai into yama-gamae position to repel an attack.*

**12**

*Bring the sai back to the left side of the waist.*

**13**

*With both sai, perform a double thrust.*

**14**

*Move the left leg into a left cat stance. Bring back both sai. Downward block.*

**15**

*Using both sai, downward block to the right.*

**16**

*Using both sai, downward block to the left.*

**17**

*Assume a one-leg position facing right. Downward block with the right sai.*

**18**

*Put the right leg down. With the right sai, upper strike.*

**19**

*Move the left leg to the front. With both sai, upper cross block.*

**20**

*Move to face the back. Starting from the down position, upper cross block with both sai.*

**21**

*Left leg sweep.*

**22**

*Change to face the front. Cross the right leg. With both sai, upper cross block.*

**23**

*Step ahead with the left leg. With both sai, downward block.*

**24**

*Step ahead with the right leg. Bring back both sai. With both sai, downward block.*

**25**

*Step ahead with the left leg. With both sai, upper cross block.*

**26**

*Pull back the left leg. Right sai upper strike.*

**27**

*Pull the right leg back diagonally to the right into a cat stance that faces the left.*

**28**

*Turn around to the right. Left reverse sai inside block.*

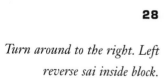

**29**

*Right reverse sai inside block to the left.*

**30**

*Return to position #3.*

**31**

*Ready position as in #2.*

**32**

*Bow.*

# SIX

# SWORD AND SAI

As with any martial art, solo performance of the kata is not enough to make an effective self-defense system. Practical application of the movements is also of utmost importance. This chapter will introduce applications of some of the movements in the basic kata presented in the previous chapters, as utilized against a sword-wielding opponent.

## Sword and Sai

Now I would like to explain the art of defense and offense using sai against a sword (Photograph 1). Stand against the sword.

1. Against a forward strike by a sword, catch the sword with upper-level cross block with both sai. At the same time, front kick with either the right or left leg (Photograph 2). Instantly thrust with both sai (Photograph 3). These are applications of basic forms 39 and 46.

2. Against a forward strike by a sword, left reverse sai upper-level block and forward thrust with the right reverse sai (Photograph 4). These are applications of basic form 10. Right after this movement, take the right foot forward shiko-dachi and thrust with the point of the right sai (Photograph 5). This is an application of number 47 of Kihongata 3.

**2**

**3**

**4**

**5**

3.  Against a forward strike by a sword, right reverse sai upper-level block, left reverse sai thrust (Photograph 6). Assume shiko-dachi and thrust with the point of the left sai (Photograph 7).

4.  Against a forward strike by a sword, left reverse sai upper block (Photograph 8). At once, strike with the right sai from the top (Photograph 9). Then thrust with the left reverse sai (Photograph 10) and right reverse sai (Photograph 11). This successive movement is an application of basic forms 26, 27, 28, and 29.

5.  Against a forward thrust by a sword, block with both sai (Photograph 12) then right sai thrust while stepping forward (Photograph 13).

**6**

**7**

**8**

**9**

**10**

**11**

**12**

**13**

# SEVEN

# BUSHI TAWADA

There was a large *Fukuju* tree in the Itosu family garden for protection against typhoons. The girth of the trunk, so wide that one could barely reach around it with both arms, bore testimony to its great age and the number of storms it had endured. Itosu made it a practice to punch the tree in lieu of a *makiwara*. As usual, he was striking the tree, which was covered by *zori*, Japanese straw sandals, with his reverse punch. Every time he struck the tree with all of his force, the seeds of the tree fell to the ground with a noise. The fist of Itosu, whose body looked like a beer barrel, was so strong that it seemed to be able to beat the stoutest man in the world. Azato, who was also referred to as a master of karate like Itosu, was astonished at the strength of Itosu's fist. They were both students of Matsumura, along with Tawada.

One day when Tawada dropped by at Itosu's, Itosu was punching the tree, whose seeds were making noise as they fell.

Tawada said to Itosu, "Your fist is as strong as usual. Nobody can endure your punch . . . well . . . except me."

Itosu stopped hitting the tree and began wiping the sweat off his face with the towel at his waist.

"Well, maybe my fist will be of no use on you. Your body is so light that you can easily elude my fists, like the wind. Hundreds of *Nisei* (youngsters) of Sanka (the collective name of three areas of Shuri, namely Toribori, Akata, and Sakiyama) couldn't catch you," Itosu said. Even Itosu acknowledged his inferiority to Tawada.

"By the way, did you know that there is a highwayman around Samu River these days?" asked Itosu.

"No," Tawada answered.

"You know, he doesn't seem to be an ordinary highwayman," Itosu continued.

"No?" Tawada inquired.

"No," Itosu kept on. "He never robs people of their money. He just challenges people to fights. He seems to use a bo. As far as I know, he has even beaten some karate experts."

"A user of the bo!" Tawada said.

"That's right," Itosu said, "and he is very good, I presume. I think he only poses as a highwayman in order to test his skills."

"Who on earth is such a master of the bo, I wonder. Do you have any idea, Itosu?" asked Tawada.

"Not at all," Itosu answered. "Rumor has it that he paints his face black, but he seems to be young."

"He must be!" Tawada interjected. "A real master of bojutsu would never do such a foolish thing! Bojutsu and karate profess the same spirit. Offense is out of the question. You should work persistently at toughening your body to protect yourself. You should aim at building up your character. I cannot forgive anyone disguising himself as a highwayman to try his skills with the bo."

"I agree. I think you can teach him a lesson," Itosu said.

"I cannot very well look the other way!"

Tawada had a very strong sense of justice, and Itosu believed that he could defeat a bo-wielding opponent, not only because he was a master of karate, but also because he was one of the best sai exponents among Matsumura's pupils. Even a very good karate exponent has difficulties in evading the flexible, straight, spearlike thrusts of the bo and the downward, swordlike attacks of the bo. Against such an attack, it is always good to be armed with some kind of weapon. Tawada was the best man for this matter, because he was a master of the sai.

A couple of nights later Tawada went over to the slope of the Samu River, where the highwayman was rumored to appear. He was carrying his favorite set of sai at his waist. The moon was very bright. Tawada had learned the sai from Matsumura, and then practiced very hard to perfect his own skill. Three years earlier, Tawada had had an encounter with Gusukuma, a master of the bo from the Tsuken school. He had never forgotten that fight, which took place on a beach. The cause of the conflict was simple: the hot-blooded students of the Tsuken school had boasted that their bojutsu was superior to everything. Upon hearing this, Tawada denied their opinion, saying that if he had his sai, he would never lose. So Gusukuma took it upon himself to challenge Tawada to prove it.

That was why they finally had a showdown. The encounter was so intense that both of them tried out their entire respective repertoire of techniques. The students of the Tsuken school and of Matsumura surrounded them.

Gusukuma stood in the *Sunakake* position (flipping sand as a distraction), with three meters between him and Tawada. Tawada, on the other hand, stood in a natural position, a sai in each hand. The observers just held their breath, waiting for some kind of movement from the combatants.

Breaking the silence, Gusukuma flicked sand at Tawada's eyes with the tip of his bo. No sooner had he done this than he tried to thrust at Tawada's chest, taking a step forward. At that moment, Tawada dodged diagonally to the left. In the next moment, turning his body to the right, Gusukuma attempted to strike Tawada in the temple with a reverse strike. Stepping to the right side, Tawada caught the bo with his right sai, held in the reverse position, and pulled Gusukuma by trapping his bo in the tines of the sai. Tawada then jabbed Gusukuma lightly in the chest with his left sai. Gusukuma groaned and collapsed.

The fight was over in an instant. Trapping the opponent's weapon in the tines of the sai was Tawada's favorite technique.

Tawada was reminiscing about his bout with Gusukuma while he waited for the showdown with the highwayman.

About one o'clock in the morning, Tawada looked around, feeling that somebody was hiding himself somewhere. Suddenly, someone jumped out from the bush on the left side of the road. Tawada tried to recognize his face in the light of the moon. The man covered his painted face with a towel, so Tawada could not easily tell who it was. He was very tall, about 180 centimeters. He blocked Tawada's way with his magnificent figure. Tawada easily recognized him as the highwayman he was looking for.

"Who are you?" Tawada asked calmly.

"I understand you must be a master of an art. I have had many fights with masters of karate and other martial arts, but have never been defeated. I practice some karate and bojutsu. I always want to try out my skills, so I am always in search of someone strong to fight with. If you don't mind, I would like to request a match with you. I will tell you my name only if you beat me. Until then I won't ask your name, and you won't ask mine, okay?" the man replied.

"All right, but I still believe that what you are doing is wrong. A true master of the art never worries about the outcome. Look at yourself! Degrading yourself in such a manner, and waiting for somebody to challenge! I understand that you must be driven by youthful ardor, but the core of the Okinawan martial arts, whether karate or bojutsu, is not found in offense. That is, its purpose is not to fight with others, not to strike others, and not to be struck by others. If you go on doing such a stupid thing, sooner or later you will get yourself killed! Besides, you are also causing a lot of anxiety among decent folks. That is very bad. I suggest that you stop this foolishness and train yourself to master the true essence of the martial arts," Tawada said.

"No more sermons! You must be a famous master. I just want to have a fight with you!" He had scarcely said this when he took up the offensive posture of *wakigamae* (the bo held at the side).

"I'm afraid there is no other way," said Tawada as he took two sai from his waist and loosely dropped both hands down with a sai in each hand, to take the natural stance, which was exactly the same posture he had employed when he fought with Gusukuma three years earlier. It is called *Mugamae* (no posture), and is for defense only.

The man slowly approached with his weapon at his side. There was nobody to interrupt. There was only the bright moon in the sky over their heads. The man was full of spirit, and his eyes, sparkling in the black face like those of a tiger or a leopard, seemed to be following the movement of his game, as if trying to catch it.

Tawada was still standing, emptying his mind. The man's stance never showed the length of his bo. Tawada recognized that the techniques of damaging downward and upward strikes as well as continuous sideward and forward strikes were favorites of the Sueyoshi school.

"You must be a student of Sueyoshi!" Before he could finish the sentence, the tip of the bo was attacking up at his chin. Tawada dodged slightly out of the way. The man attempted a downward strike at Tawada's head as he moved one step closer, but Tawada caught it with his right sai, held in the reverse grip. The fight was over in only a second. The opponent dropped his bo and knelt down, clutching his chest with both hands. He groaned, suffering for a moment. After a moment, he stood up again.

"You've won. You are the strongest man I've ever met. You must be a very famous master. I apologize for my rudeness. As you have already pointed out, I have studied the art of the Sueyoshi school. My name is Iba. But I have never been taught by Master Sueyoshi. I was taught by Gushi, a student of Master Sueyoshi . . . well . . . it was not really a teaching, but a mere imitation of the art. So for the most part, I have been practicing on my own—very hard, though. Gradually, I became conceited, overestimating my own skill, I'm afraid, and found myself challenging people on the road. Today I learned a lesson about how frightening it is to challenge people on the road. I am very thankful that I was not killed, though you could have done it. I will stop this foolishness for good and try harder to see the core of bojutsu, as you have suggested. Well . . . would you please tell me your name?" he finally asked.

"I am very glad that you understand. My name is Tawada. You should not forget that the martial arts are only for training yourself," Tawada replied.

"You are the famous Master Tawada?" Iba said in surprise, and kept saying, "I am truly sorry. Please forgive me," he begged, kneeling down on the spot and making himself very flat on the ground, in the Japanese manner of profound apology.

After that, Iba became a student of Tawada, and through hard training was able to master the core of the martial arts.

# EIGHT
# BUSHI MATSUMURA

Everyone who practices karate has heard the name of Bushi Matsumura. No doubt, he was one of the originators of modern karate. The masters of karate, specifically *Shuri-te* (Shuri is a city in Okinawa), such as Itosu, Azato, Mayuna, Chibana, Tawada, Ishimine, Chinen, Itarashiki, Aragaki, Kinjo, Sueyoshi, and Kuwae, among others, were all students of Matsumura. Surprisingly, it is little known that Matsumura was a master of saijutsu as well as karate. His karate teacher was Wai Xinxian, a Chinese military officer. Matsumura himself tried very hard to master the sai.

Commodore Matthew C. Perry called at the port of Okinawa in 1853 when he arrived in Japan with his U.S. navy fleet for the first time. At that time, King

Sho Ko invited him to the castle. Matsumura was the instructor for the king. A little over forty, he was in the prime of his manhood. The question posed to King Sho Ko by Perry was: "I have heard that Okinawan martial arts do not employ any weapons. Would you mind introducing some masters?"

Upon hearing this request, the king answered "There is one."

Perry got very interested. "Who is this master, Your Highness?"

"He is my instructor, Matsumura Sokon."

"Is he good?" Perry continued.

"Oh yes, he is the best in Okinawa. He is also smart. He is good. On top of that, his wife is the most beautiful woman in Okinawa, just as he is the best karate man, you see. She is madly in love with him. He is very strong."

"Oh, karate. That must be the martial art that does not employ any weapons," Perry said.

"That's right," the king replied. "He is a master of this art. I practice with him."

Perry showed more interest. "Well, I want to meet him. Would you mind?"

After hearing Perry's request, the king ordered his man to call Matsumura. Before long, Matsumura came up in front of him.

"Your Highness . . . " he said.

"Well, Mr. Perry wants to see karate. Can you demonstrate?" the king asked.

Perry noticed the strong body of Matsumura. Matsumura answered, "Yes, I can demonstrate one kata."

He stood up and took his place. He bowed toward the king and Perry, then took the ready stance. He looked dignified. Everybody in the castle compound watched him without a word. Matsumura's body movement was quick, his limbs like lightning. The demonstration was over in about a minute. The kata he performed was *Wankan*. It was, of course, the first time Perry had seen karate. The demonstration had spiritual beauty and strength. He gave Matsumura a very big hand as Matsumura bowed and prepared to leave.

"Karate has strength and beauty. It is like art in motion. I wonder how karate is employed in a real match. Your Highness, if you really don't mind, I would like to see him fight a match with one of my men. His name is Scott, and he is the strongest man in our crew. He is so strong he could kill a bull," Perry urged the king.

"Very well." The king's answer was too simple. He again made a request of Matsumura. "Mr. Perry wants you to have a match with one of his men. His name is Scott. Go and make it a point of honor to go through this thing for me."

The king was fond of this type of thing. He was sometimes driven by youthful vigor. When the king was a boy, he was practicing karate with Matsumura one day. The king was so conceited about his technique that he tried to deliver a *Nidan-geri* (jumping double front kick) to Matsumura. Matsumura, recognizing the proud nature of his student, decided to teach him a lesson and show him his weakness and conceit. Matsumura struck the king's powerful kick with *Shuto* (knife-hand) strikes. The king lost his balance and fell to the ground. He became so angry with Matsumura that as punishment, he confined him to his quarters.

Now, Matsumura thought that what he had expected had come. He knew that the king would never be satisfied with only a demonstration of kata. Matsumura recalled a rumor that in the Western world there was a martial art that resembled karate and utilized the fists, but he really couldn't tell what it was. What's more, fighting with a Westerner was really out of the question because the point to victory was to know the opponent first. It is very dangerous to fight someone whom you don't know.

Scott seemed to be a guard for Perry. Scott proceeded to the front of the king and Perry, and nodded to them. He was over two meters tall, and very muscular. He looked very strong. On the other hand, Matsumura was only about 170 centimeters tall. He was not a short man for the standard in Japan at the time, but when he stood against Scott, they looked like an adult and a child.

Everybody thought that Matsumura was sure to lose. Matsumura had the same feeling. Scott appeared to be a powerful opponent.

Matsumura was recalling a fight with another karate master, Uehara. At that time, he thought that his opponent was very strong. So he decided to fight to the last, only hoping that his last would be true to his name. He stood, harmonizing with the universe. He stood straight and firm, coercing his opponent with the power of the universe. Uehara became afraid before Matsumura and couldn't do anything but kneel.

Scott must be stronger than Uehara. Again, Matsumura thought the same thing that he did when he faced Uehara. And again he decided to sacrifice his life.

At this stage, Matsumura found harmony between himself and the universe, as well as with Scott. Scott approached with his hands forward. Matsumura stood in the *Neko-ashi-dachi* (cat stance) with his left arm forward and his right fist near his left elbow. Scott punched at Matsumura's face like a gust of wind. Matsumura, like a streamer or flag in the wind, evaded the punch. Matsumura was still facing his opponent with his left arm forward and his right fist near his left elbow.

Matsumura changed his position, moving to the left. Scott struck in vain at Matsumura's face without pause. Every time Scott tried to strike Matsumura, Matsumura's body moved to the right or left, like a flag blowing in the wind. The distance between the two combatants made no difference from the onset. Scott's machine-gun-like fists never caught Matsumura. Scott's face showed irritation and frustration, as well as impatience. He seemed to want to beat Matsumura to death one way or another. Scott forgot about his defense in order to defeat Matsumura. On the other hand, Matsumura could see the movement of his opponent's body as well as of his mind, like the shadow of the moon on the waveless surface of a pond. For Matsumura, there was no such thing as the opponent. He was only moving as naturally as possible. This movement was the reflection of his daily practice, which flowed like a stream of water. Scott became tired from his furious attack. All of the spectators, including King Sho Ko and

Perry, were surprised at Matsumura's skillful *Tai-sabaki* (body evasion), contrary to their expectation that the fight would be a very furious one.

The vexed Scott seemed to give up punching and tried to grab Matsumura in order to throw him down. He tried to approach one way or another, with both hands defenselessly opened. At this point, Scott abandoned legitimate martial arts in order to win. He was acting totally wild and crazed. As soon as Scott's large body loomed over Matsumura's, Matsumura changed his fighting style from swinging and dodging to step firmly forward and punch with his right fist into the pit of Scott's stomach, like a bolt of lightning. Scott's big body slowly fell forward to the ground, where he remained motionless.

All of the spectators, including the king and Perry, seemed as if they were waking from a dream, and clapped their hands violently. Matsumura punched Scott in the pit of his stomach again, this time just enough to revive him.

Perry said to the king, "As you said, he is a master of karate. Even Scott was treated like a baby."

The king replied, "I think this fight was an example of technique versus power."

"I think he would be undefeatable against an unarmed opponent," Perry said. "But suppose someone armed with weapons were to challenge him? Do you think Matsumura would use any weapons?"

"Well, I think he would probably use something," the king answered.

"What?" Perry inquired.

"It depends upon what the opponent uses," the king said.

"If he uses a sword or something," Perry persistently inquired.

"I think he would use the sai," answered the king.

"Sai . . . what kind of weapon is that?" Perry asked again.

"The sai is an iron weapon that has U-shaped handles where you entwine your fingers. You can hold them in both hands and manipulate them freely," the king explained.

"I would very much like to see them, Your Highness. Do you use the same kind of forms as in karate?" Perry asked.

"Yes, I can have Matsumura demonstrate."

"Oh, I would really appreciate that," Perry said excitedly.

The king instantly ordered Matsumura, saying "Matsumura, Mr. Perry would like to see the sai. Why don't you show us a kata?"

"Certainly," he answered, and asked one of the king's men to fetch a pair of sai, then proceeded to the position where he had demonstrated the karate kata earlier. Holding a sai in each hand, he bowed, and as he had done earlier with the karate kata, he started to move to and fro, left and right. He manipulated the sai like his own hands, striking with the grips or points, and sweeping them. They seemed to stick fast to his hands. The demonstration was an exquisite show of skill, astonishing everyone in attendance. In about one minute, the demonstration was over. The kata he displayed was his own original one.

"Wonderful, truly amazing. Like karate, I would also like to see how the sai would be used in an actual situation. How about having him fight against somebody using a sword? But it would be a life or death struggle," Perry considered.

"Matsumura would surely beat him. Besides, the real purpose of karate or saijutsu is to protect ourselves. Therefore, he will not be harmed, or even punched, I suspect," King Sho Ko answered confidently.

"Is that so? Well, Your Highness, we have a master of the sword. His name is Richard, and his family have been sword masters for generations in England. He himself is undefeated. He is also my personal teacher, as well as a man of character. He would be a good match for Matsumura. Would you mind their having a match, Your Highness?" Perry kept on. "Of course, with swords, one of them might be killed or injured. But, I still suggest, Your Highness, that they have a match, making it a point of honor for both the Ryukyu martial arts and American martial arts."

Even at the end of the Edo era, King Sho Ko, his karate teacher Matsumura Sokon, as well as other warriors, had the mindset of *Bushido* in their blood, cultivated from the era of civil strife. And their minds were so pure that they happily devoted their lives to their masters' orders. Likewise, Perry's men had the same spirit of chivalry, cultivated through the Western martial traditions. They also had loyalty to their commander, Perry, even to the point of dying for him.

The king ordered Matsumura to face Richard, while Perry instructed Richard to face Matsumura. Neither man disobeyed his orders. They decided to face each other like true warriors, in order to inquire into the core of true martial arts.

Matsumura thought that this time—unlike the fight with Scott, in which neither of them had any weapons—he had to expect to fare much worse. He was facing a master of the sword. He had fought with many sword masters. He recalled one encounter he had had with a master of Jigenryu, Ijuin Hayato, which he had never forgotten. Hayato was a warrior from Satsuma (the former name for the southern area of Kyushu now known as Kagoshima). He was a retainer of Sakamoto Tatewaki, a high-ranking officer of the Ryukyu branch of the Shogunate. He learned his art from Togo Gensai. The officer Sakamoto Tatewaki wanted that fight as badly as Perry wanted one today. At that time, Sakamoto only wanted to see a good fight between Ijuin, master of Jigenryu and the teacher of martial arts for the Ryukyuan king, Matsumura, who was often rumored to be the number one karate man in the entire Ryukyu kingdom. Sakamoto suggested this fight just out of curiosity. It was just lucky that the king had a chance to see it as well.

The encounter took place at the king's palace. At that time, Matsumura stood against Ijuin's sword with his sai in his hands. Ijuin assumed the *Tonbo no Kamae* (dragonfly posture), a guard that originated in Jigenryu. He closed the distance to Matsumura by slowly advancing, determined to cut deeply into

Matsumura's shoulder. The spectators trembled as if they themselves were about to be killed. However, Matsumura remained cool, his sai held in his dangling hands. Matsumura harmonized with his opponent, and left him to the natural course of his movement. He seemed to be calmly determined, as if jumping into the fire where there was nothing, no life or death, just harmony. Ijuin's burning spirit was diminished by Matsumura's calmness, and his sword missed the mark completely, caught firmly by both sai. Matsumura's body was now very close to Ijuin, and the slightest movement by Ijuin would have meant being impaled on the sai, which were now held at his chest and throat. Recognizing his defeat, Ijuin shouted, "You've got me there!" The conflict lasted only a minute. It was really a miracle that Matsumura never let the master of Jigenryu touch him, placed the opponent under his control, and won without serious injury to either party. The king was impressed with the technique. Since that time, King Sho Ko had trusted Matsumura more than any other of his men. That was why he was so confident that Matsumura would be neither killed nor injured when Perry issued the challenge.

Before the fight, Matsumura was really determined, and ready to die. *In the beginning there was nothing. My life and even death is in the atoms,* Matsumura thought. The atoms were in nothing. Everything was in nothing. The point of this, indeed of all of his beliefs, was to harmonize with all creatures. The ultimate truth of the martial arts is to harmonize with the opponent. You can never go against or resist his movement. Just move according to his actions. Matsumura practiced every day to master this.

Seeing Richard hold his sword, Matsumura thought that they shared the same atoms. They were never separate molecules. They were harmonized with the universe. There was nothing but harmony.

Matsumura stood against Richard with his sai rising. He was above winning or losing. Richard had devoted his entire life to his sword, and had fought many duels, in which he had never been defeated. Richard was also big, but at

190 centimeters, he was not as large as Scott. His sharp eyes scared everybody because he had mastered not only his weapon, but his life and death as well.

In Richard's mind there seemed to be a determination not to be defeated. Defeat meant death for him. He had to kill Matsumura. He always had the same thoughts when facing his opponents. Richard's intensity was like an elephant trying to stomp on an ant, or a lion that attacked a rabbit with all its might.

Richard unsheathed his sword and pointed it at Matsumura's chest. This was, of course, the first time Matsumura had seen a Western swordsman's stance. He couldn't tell what kind of attack might issue from that stance. Matsumura held his left sai to the front and his right sai over his head, like the stance in the karate kata *Pinan Yondan*.

Matsumura was determined to harmonize with his opponent's movement, which meant an *Ai-uchi* or simultaneous strike. That was the stance used to correspond to the another's movement. If the opponent remained still, so did he. If the opponent moved slightly so did he, but a little faster, to make the fight a decisive one.

First, Richard wanted to stab Matsumura through the chest, but Matsumura's stance as well as his spirit nailed him to the spot. This was the first time since his first duel that Richard had encountered an opponent of Matsumura's caliber. Matsumura's posture showed that he was ready to die by Ai-uchi. At the moment Richard stabbed Matsumura, Richard would also be killed. Waiting for that moment, Matsumura held his right sai over his head, in order to throw it into the chest of his opponent like a *shuriken*.

Richard lost his timing to launch a decisive offensive at Matsumura. And because he lost his timing, he couldn't attack. Matsumura's face showed nothing, no fear, no delusion. He was thinking only that when Richard tried to stab him, he would just throw the sai in his right hand. This movement would only take a second. A second would decide his fate. The expression on his face showed that he was above the matter of life and death.

Both of them remained still for a long time. For Richard, Matsumura's sai and his mind, as well, were a hindrance. It seemed strange to Richard that Matsumura's body seemed completely covered by the left sai. Richard thought that even if he tried to stab Matsumura, his strike would be blocked by the left sai, but Matsumura could still counterattack with the right-hand sai.

Richard admitted his defeat, both technically and mentally. He could not stand still anymore, feeling the greasy sweat all over his body. He shouted, "You've won, Mr. Matsumura!" All of the spectators gave Matsumura a very big hand. He was beyond the mastery of karate and *kobudo*. He had mastered the essence of the martial arts.

# About the Author

Murakami Katsumi was born in Fukuoka Prefecture in 1927. He has trained in *jujutsu, kenpo, karatedo,* Ryukyu *Kobudo,* and Chinese *quanfa.* In 1973, he was invited by the *Goju-kai Karatedo* Australia Branch to give an introduction to *Karatedo* and Ryukyu *Kobudo.* He is licensed in *Shorinryu karatedo* as *Hanshi 9-dan,* and holds a *Shihan* license in *Tō'onryu karatedo, Shihan* in Ryukyu *Kobudo,* and an instructor's license in Chinese *Quanfa (Taijiquan, Xingyiquan,* and *Baguazhang).* Through diligent, hard training in *karate* and *kenpo,* he aims at harmonious, balanced training for both the body and the spirit. He advocates martial arts training to unify the mind and body. As the head of the Shorinkan Dojo, he is engaged in teaching and promoting the martial arts. Other books by the author in Japanese include *Karatedo to Ryukyu Kobudo (Karatedo and Ancient*

*Ryukyu Martial Arts), Ryukyu Bojutsu,* (Staff Fighting of Ryukyu), *Karate no Kokoro to Waza (The Spirit and Technique of Karate), and Ryukyu Bojutsu no Higi (Secret Techniques of Ryukyu Bojutsu).* He resides in Tagawa City, Fukuoka.